Embracing Life

Poems that inspire
the heart and soul

Dolores:
I hope the poems in
this book inspire you.
Florida

By: Florida Vigil

First published by Dog Ear Publishing
4010 W. 86th Street, Ste H
Indianapolis, IN 46268
www.dogearpublishing.net

ISBN: 978-160844-126-6
Library of Congress Control Number: 2009938787

This book is printed on acid-free paper.

Printed in the United States of America

Embracing Life is dedicated ...

to my husband George and my daughter Georgette
who have always been there for me.

To my brother Thomas, who passed away of lung
cancer in 2005. He was my inspiration.

To my mother Ruth, who passed away in 2007.
Her love was unconditional.

Embracing Life

Embracing Life, is a poetry book about taking life into your own hands and living the very best life that you can. Live each day as if it was your last day. Cherish each moment. Life is priceless. Don't take life for granted. Life passes by so quickly. Make things happen today. Focus on the positive instead of the negative. Make a difference in someone's life; be compassionate, considerate, and reach out to someone in need.

Open up your heart to the Lord and believe in the Lord. Miracles happen when you put your trust in the Lord. Take time to see the beauty in life. Sometimes we are in such a hurry that we don't stop to see the beauty that surrounds us. Spend time with family. Hold family close to the heart. Memories live in the heart forever.

To embrace life is to evaluate your life today, and decide what is important. Find happiness in what you do and open up your heart to all possibilities.

Contents

Introduction

As I get older, I embrace life even more than I did before. Life has become more precious. I take time to enjoy the beauty around me. Life has more meaning. I worry less about past mistakes and live in the present. I treasure each moment of my life.

I find a lot of comfort in giving instead of receiving. I find inner peace in prayer and meditation. Instead of rushing through life, I have become more patient and realize that not everything has to be done right now. When I wake up in the morning, I give thanks to the Lord for a new day, for giving me life, for family, and for friends.

I thank God for giving me hope and faith and for the strength to be able to do the things I enjoy doing.

It has become so much easier for me to apologize to someone so that I can have peace in my heart.

I have learned not to take life so seriously, and I am able to accept constructive criticism more easily. I believe life is a gift from heaven above, and I will continue to embrace life to the fullest.

Embracing life has inspired the poems in this book and is demonstrated in the chapters: Beauty, Life, Love, Family, and Prayer. I am pleased to share these experiences that are universal and may encourage you to understand more about your own life's journey.

Beauty

Give thanks
to the Lord
for the Beauty of Life

The Beauty Of Life

The beauty of life is to live each day as if it is your last day.
Embrace each day.
Don't spend time dwelling on past mistakes.
Start each day anew.
Reach for the stars.
Make your dreams come true.
Live each day to the fullest.
Don't let life pass you by.
Make things happen today.
Appreciate what God has given to you, and make the most of every day.
Stop and smell the roses.
Focus on giving instead of receiving and you will experience the beauty of life.
Look around you, so much beauty to behold.
God has created a new day.
Take time to enjoy every moment.
> The sunrise
> The blue sky
> The mountains
> The falling rain
> The sunset

Don't spend time thinking of what the future may bring and what possessions you may acquire.
Count your blessings today.
Give of yourself unconditionally.
Don't take life for granted.
Give thanks to the Lord for the beauty of life.

Flowers

Flowers so beautiful, fragrant, sweet, and oh so colorful.
You intoxicate my senses.
You take my breath away.
I can't decide which ones are my favorites: sweet williams,
poppies, carnations, or roses, to name a few.
So many exquisite colors, shapes, and sizes.
Some grow in the sun, others in the shade.
Some need a lot of care, others don't.
You grow so freely in my garden.
Some attract bees, butterflies, and hummingbirds.
You bring so much beauty and happiness: on birthdays,
weddings, Valentine's Day, and so many holidays.
You are all unique in your own special way.
Some bloom in early spring, summer, or all season long,
until the snow falls.
Your beauty lasts a lifetime in my heart.

Springtime

It's springtime in the Rockies.
My heart is filled with anticipation.
Take out your umbrella.
I hear the rain falling against the window pane.
The tulips and daffodils are in full bloom.
The birds are chirping.
The grass is green.
The children are out playing.
The whole world has come alive.
Oh, beautiful springtime, I wish you were here to stay.

My Flower Garden

When I wake up in the morning, my flower garden seems
to call for me.
As I go into my flower garden, my flowers seem to greet
me with "good morning."
They seem to smile at me.
So many different colors, sizes, and scents.
I weed the garden, give the flowers water, greet them with
"hello," and a smile.
So many memories and dreams are formed as I walk
through my flower garden.
My flowers are always happy, never sad.
They give me so much beauty and happiness.
Butterflies stop by to say hello.
I wish my flowers could always be in full bloom.
The season is now changing, and we must say goodbye.
My flowers will be in full bloom again next year.
My dear friends, your beauty will warm my heart through
the cold winter months.

Secret Garden

Come to me and take my hand.
Lead me to the secret garden, where you and I can share
our thoughts.
Let's pack a picnic basket and enjoy this beautiful summer
day.
Let's sit on the wooden bench by the day lilies, where we
can make new memories as we observe the beauty that
surrounds us.
Can you hear the trickle of the water fountain?
See the beautiful butterflies, smell the sweet, fragrant, col-
orful flowers, and see those doves flying up ahead.
Let's retire to the chairs by the floral background and enjoy
the closeness that we once shared.
Let's hold hands and let our minds wander to another time
and place when you and I were like one.

Valentine's Day

Valentine's Day, a day for lovers,
beautiful, fragrant flowers, sparkling diamonds,
sweetheart candy, Valentine cards, soft music, a day to
spend with you, my love.
A quiet dinner for two, by candlelight.
Holding hands, gazing into each other's eyes.
A sweet kiss, listening to our favorite music.
A glass of champagne,
just sitting close by you,
saying, "I love you,"
makes it a special Valentine's Day.

Life

Life's highway
is a lifetime
journey

Life's Highway

We must all travel life's highway.
Life's highway is a lifetime journey.
How we travel life's highway is entirely up to us.
We must make choices along the way.
We may encounter many hardships and stormy weather.
At times the road may seem rocky.
There is no turning back once the journey begins.
As I travel life's highway, I prefer to take the scenic route.
Stop and enjoy the beautiful, fragrant flowers, the mountains, the falling rain, the blue sky, the warmth of the sun, the stars, and the moon.
I will stop and take in all the beauty that life has to offer.
At times I may stop and dream along the way, wipe someone's tears, help the less fortunate than me, spread some laughter and joy, and open up my heart to others.
I want to travel with a positive attitude and make a difference.
How I travel life's highway is entirely up to me; when I reach my destination is up to the Lord.

If I Could Fly

If I could fly, I would soar like an eagle.
I would sit on the mountain top and look down at the city.
I would fly like a kite, so high I would reach the sky.
I would feel the wind on my wings as I fly higher and higher.
I would fly through the clouds and feel their softness against my wings.
I would fly on a rainy day and feel the raindrops on my wings.
I would fly, fly, fly, until the rainbows appeared.
I would fly all day and night.
I would fly by the light of the moon and count the stars.
I would fly until I reached paradise, my destination.

Start Living

Hop on the train, don't be late.
The world is moving.
The world will not stand still for you.
Don't waste another moment start living your life.
What's holding you back?
The world is changing so fast, don't stay behind.
Experience all the wonderful things that life has to offer.
Open yourself to all possibilities.
There is no time like the present to start living your life.
Make new memories today, don't waste any time.
Live for today.
Don't wait until tomorrow, tomorrow may never come.

Memories

It's not the designer clothes you wear, the jewels you pos-
sess,
the luxury car you drive, or the million dollar house you live
in,
that you will be remembered by when you leave this world.
You will be remembered by the love you give, the kindness
you show,
your smile, the way you hold someone's hand, the hugs
you give,
the quality time you spend with someone, and all the gifts
you give
from the heart.
The memories you leave behind are the treasures that will
be held close to someone's heart, and there is nothing
more precious than that.
So, my friend, set your priorities straight and evaluate your
life today.
Start making memories that last a lifetime.

Don't Be Afraid

Don't be afraid to reach out to someone, to take the time to
lend a helping hand.
Now is the time to make peace with someone, to apolo-
gize, and to open up your heart to forgiveness.
Don't be afraid to give someone a second chance.
Don't be afraid of rejection.
Come with love in your heart and someone will know you
are sincere.
Open up your heart and show someone you care.
Don't wait another moment to be there for someone.
The peace and joy you feel in your heart will last a lifetime.
There is nothing more beautiful than to see someone's
smile, to feel someone's touch, or to hear someone say,
"Thank you."
If you can make someone's life a little easier, count your
blessings.
Don't expect recognition; the only reward is to fill some-
one's heart with joy, and that is the most beautiful gift that
they will treasure.
Don't wait for someone to call on you,
make the first move.
Don't be afraid to open up your heart to someone today.

Footprints In The Snow

It is a cold winter day.
You look out the window.
Snow is falling.
You decide to go for a walk.
As you walk, tears fill your eyes.
It is so cold!
The tears freeze on your cheeks.
Your mind wanders to the day when you met him.
You were high school sweethearts, young and innocent.
You promised to love each other until the end of time.
Your families thought your love would not last, but your love was real and magical.
You had been together for a long time when God decided to take him to heaven.
You felt like your life was over.
Time stood still.
There seemed to be nothing left to live for.
As you continue to walk, you think of the beautiful relationship you had.
Your heart aches for him.
Sometimes you don't think you can go on.
You walk for a long time.
The snow is so cold on your feet.
All of a sudden, you hear footsteps behind you.
You turn around and see an extra set of footprints in the snow.
You hear a voice.
You see an elderly gentleman with long hair and a beard.
The gentleman has a halo around his head.
He is followed by lambs.
It's an unbelievable sight!
The elderly gentleman speaks in a soft voice.
He says, "You are going through a difficult time now.

There will be brighter days ahead.
Remember my child, God gives, and God takes away.
Live for today.
Stop worrying about what could have been, and accept
life's circumstances.
Live today as if it is your last day.
Miracles do happen."
All of a sudden, the elderly gentleman and the lambs dis-
appear.
Your mind wanders back to the present time, did you imag-
ine all that?
But you can still see an extra set of footprints in the snow.
Even though it is cold, you feel such warmth flow through
your body.
You know then that from this moment on, your life will be
full of promise.
God is watching over you.

Listen To Your Heart

Listen to your heart.
Your heart is trying to tell you that even though you have
been hurt before, it's time to love once again.
You have felt the pain of losing love, but you can't go on
mistrusting forever.
Take a chance at love.
Your heart is telling you to take it one day at a time and to
see where love will lead you.
Let your heart tell you what to do.
Your heart will tell you no lie,
it will not lead you astray,
it will lead you in the right direction.
Your heart is telling you that this time it is true love and to
open up your heart to happiness.
If you follow your heart, your dreams will come true.

Alone

Why do I feel so alone?
I wake up in the morning feeling blue.
I know I have so much to live for.
I have you in my life,
I have wonderful friends,
a great job,
but loneliness always seems to follow me.
I go through the motions of life.
I take care of myself and others.
I smile, I greet people, and I seem to be happy.
Other people envy my positive attitude and my sense of
humor.
They wonder where I get my energy.
I am looking for something, but I don't know what.
There is an aching, empty feeling in my heart that I can't
explain.
I spend a lot of time alone.
Sometimes I wonder what life is all about.
Where will I go from here?
I miss you when you are gone.
I wish we could spend more time together.
When you are gone, the house seems so empty.
I always look forward to spending time with you.
I have so much to do, but there is an emptiness that
lingers on.
Maybe I am spending too much time alone.

You Were There

When I was down and out and there seemed to be no light
at the end of the tunnel,
        You were there.
When my heart was aching and the skies were gray,
        you were there.
When my life was empty and there seemed to be no one
there for me,
        you were there.
When I was lonely and felt that I could not go on,
        you were there.
When the nights were long and I could not sleep,
        you were there.
When I needed someone to talk to, when I needed a
helping hand and a shoulder to lean on,
        you were there.
You were my support system.
You showed compassion beyond belief.
My friend, you are my hero.
You have always been there for me.

You Can Count On Me

I look at your face, and I see sadness that I have never
seen before.
Your eyes have a faraway look.
The other day, I saw tears in your eyes.
I know something is not right with you.
Open up your heart and let me in.
I am here for you.
You probably think that no one can understand the pain
that you are going through and that you can work out
everything alone.
You can count on me.
Don't cry, my friend.
Nothing is impossible when you have someone by your
side to help carry the burden.
There are brighter days ahead.
Even after the rain, there are rainbows.
Life is so much easier when there is someone to confide
in, to hold your hand, and to wipe away the tears.
Soon you will smile again.
There will be no more tears.
Time has a way of healing the pain and making us
stronger.
I am not here to lecture nor to give advice.
I am here to sit by your side, to listen, and to make your life
a little easier.
My friend, I brought you a dozen roses to cheer you up.

Don't Wait Too Long

Don't bring me flowers when I am gone,
bring me flowers now that I can smell the flowers, arrange
them in a vase, and enjoy their beauty.
Don't cry for me when I am gone,
sit with me now.
Let's reminisce and shed a few tears together.
Don't think of what you could have done for me,
do those things for me now.
Take time to pour me a cup of coffee,
help me with those things I am not able to do.
Don't say kind words about me when I am gone, say those
kind words now that I am able to hear them.
Don't think of all the time we could have spent together,
spend time with me now.
Don't say you are too busy to talk, call me on the tele-
phone.
Open up your heart, I am listening.
Don't say you wish you could have been there for me.
I waited to see your sweet face,
I needed your company, and I needed your touch.
I spend many lonely nights all alone,
thinking of you, wondering when you will come.
Don't think of the hugs and kisses you should have given
me,
hug and kiss me now.
I need your closeness and your sweet embrace.
I need to hear your voice.
I need your love now.
Don't wait too long to say, "I love you,"
it might be too late.

If I Were An Artist

If I were an artist, I would paint a picture of you.
I would capture your beauty on canvas.
I would paint your big, brown eyes that sparkle when you look at me.
Your sweet lips that kiss me so tenderly, your beautiful smile that makes my heart skip a beat.
Your fingers that touch me so gently and your strong arms that hold me when I am feeling lonely.
As an artist, I would only focus on your outer beauty.
The wonderful qualities that you possess, I would not be able to capture on canvas.
Your voice that sounds like a melody when you speak my name, your wonderful sense of humor, your positive attitude, your honesty, your sincerity, and your generosity.
These are special qualities that can only be captured in my heart.

Priceless

A hello, how are you?
A genuine smile,
A tender touch,
A hug,
A helping hand,
A telephone call,
Sitting together holding hands.
The flowers you bring,
Sharing a snack,
Conversing with you,
The consideration you show.
Taking a walk,
Looking at the mountains,
watching the sunrise and the sunset.
The way you say my name.
Just sitting quietly together,
without saying a word is priceless to me.

Where Are You Going?

Where are you going, my friend, in such a hurry?
Take a walk, stop and smell the roses.
Stop and say hello.
How many projects are you working on?
Are you going to finish one?
Take time to meditate.
Pamper yourself,
take a bubble bath,
just sit down and relax.
What is important to you?
Visit a friend, take a nap.
Visit a spa, get a manicure, a pedicure.
Enjoy a night out with family and friends.
Life passes by so fast.
Set your priorities straight.
Make a decision today.
What is important in life?
Leave your worries behind.
Slow down, live your life.

Wall Flower

Who do you see when you look at yourself in the mirror?
Do you see someone who is afraid to try new things, afraid
you will not succeed?
Someone who is afraid to express herself, smart but not
sure of herself, lacking confidence and afraid not to be
accepted.
Someone who is afraid to come out and show the world
who she really is, afraid to take a chance?
You wish you could reach out to others, but you hold back,
you lack confidence.
You always sit in the back row, afraid to be called on.
That handsome guy you dream of just smiled at you, you
smiled back.
Your heart is beating fast, your palms are sweating, you
walk fast, afraid if he talks to you, you might get tongue-
tied.
The school dance is coming up, you dream of going, but
you are afraid to ask someone. Stop dreaming, take a
chance, stand tall, don't be shy, be assertive, be strong.
It's about time you take a good look at yourself.
You have so much to offer.
Come out of your shell, before life passes you by.

Teardrops

I thought that after awhile there would be no more tears.
That time would heal the pain.
This morning I woke up and just the thought of you brought
the tears flowing.
I don't know how long it takes to forget you, maybe a life-
time?
My life seems so empty without you.
The thought of you,
the mention of your name,
and the memories of your sweet face bring teardrops to my
eyes.
How many teardrops must I cry before the pain goes
away?

Missing You

You never know how much you miss someone until they
are gone.
You miss their voice, their smile, and their tender touch.
The pain you feel inside your heart lingers on.
You miss the way they called your name and the way they
held your hand.
You long to see their face, to feel their hand in yours, and
to see the sparkle in their eyes.
When you cry, they are not here to wipe the tears from
your eyes and to ask, "What is wrong?"
You hurt so bad you feel you are going mad.
You ask yourself, "*What can I do?*"
Even though they are not here, you feel their presence.
You hold their memories close to your heart.

Mourn

I will mourn for you in my own way, even if it takes a lifetime. When I mention your name and no one seems to care and the world has forgotten you, I hold you close to my heart.

When I hear your favorite music, I remember how you loved to dance and how you swayed to the music.

When I eat at your favorite restaurant, I remember the food you liked to eat and the wonderful conversations we had.

When I pass by a flower shop, I stop to buy you a bouquet of flowers, then I remember you are not here.

When I go shopping, I stop to look at clothes, and I want to pick out an outfit for you, then I remember you are not here.

When I go to the beauty shop, I picture you sitting there getting your hair cut, and tears fill my eyes.

When I get up in the morning, and when I go to bed at night, I think of you. Sometimes I can hear you call my name. You may not be here, but you are always on my mind and in my heart. When I close my eyes, I picture your face and beautiful smile.

I will mourn for you until the end of time. You are in my heart to stay.

Childhood Days

How grand it would be to be a child again,
no stress, no problems, no cares.
Playing outside on a summer day, with my brothers and
sisters.
Riding a bike as fast as the wind.
Playing baseball with my friends.
Walking to school, mom holding my hand.
Jumping rope and counting out loud.
Swinging on the swing and day dreaming.
Baking gingersnap cookies with mom.
Picking wildflowers out in the fields for mom and seeing
her beautiful smile.
Playing catch with my dog, Fido.
Doing my homework with my best friend, Agnes.
Telling my best friend secrets.
Having a crush on that nice boy, Eugene.
Mom reading me the story Snow White.
Going fishing with dad, catching butterflies, flying a kite
with my sister, Bernice.
Horseback riding out in the country.
Oh! How I would like to relive my wonderful childhood
days.
The memories of the carefree days when I was a child
make me smile and feel nostalgic.

Unique

I am like no one else.
I am unique in my own way.
Let me be myself.
Look at me, who do you see?
My smile, the sound of my voice, the way I walk, my touch,
and the special things I do are like no one else.
I don't want to be like anyone else.
I am an individual with unique qualities.
When I speak, don't interrupt, let me express myself in my
own special way.
Don't criticize me, compliment me on my accomplish-
ments.
Don't take me for granted.
Accept me the way I am.
Let me be that unique person in your life, and I will love
you forever in my own special way.

Inadequate

I think that the feeling of inadequacy stems from childhood.
When you grow up being told that you never do anything
right and are constantly criticized, you feel like you never
measure up.
You try so hard to please others.
You want to be perfect, but the feeling of inadequacy is
always there.
You are the best at everything you do, but you always feel
empty inside.
It is very difficult to accept a compliment,
because you think you don't deserve it.
You go through life trying to please others and to get their
approval.
I think that parents ought to praise their children on their
accomplishments and let them know how wonderful they
are.
Even when they fail, parents ought to be there to give them
encouragement, to praise them for trying and for doing the
very best they can.

Merry-Go-Round

Round and round goes the merry-go-round, much like life.
So fast it feels like a whirlwind.
I feel so dizzy.
Goes on and on from early morning to late at night.
I don't seem to know where I am going.
I can't get my feet on the ground.
So many thoughts go through my mind.
I feel like crying.
My heart is beating a mile a minute.
I feel all wound up as I listen to the sound of the hounds.
My life continues to go round and round like a merry-go-round.
What is my destination?
Will I ever get there?
I have no confidence, no desires, and no will to go on.
I can't find peace.
I know I must let go of this craziness, or my life will continue to go round and round until I gain control.

Pain

Since you've been gone, there is an endless pain in my heart.
The pain is so deep it takes my breath away.
It feels like a dagger digging right into my soul.
It affects my whole being.
It stops me in my tracks.
I can't think.
I feel like I am sinking.
The whole world keeps moving on, while I am at a stand-still.
I don't seem to be able to get hold of myself.
It hurts so bad, I feel so sad.
No matter where I go, or what I do, the pain goes on and on.
At times I feel like I am going insane.
I cry out, but no one hears me.
I have to be brave and put on a front.
I know I have to move on, but the memories of you continue to haunt my heart and soul.
I wish you were here, my love.
I miss you so desperately.

The Night

When the night is dreary and you see only darkness, I will
be there for you.
When you are feeling all alone and it feels like no one
cares, call my name, and I will come running to you.
When your heart is aching and the pain seems to pierce
right through your soul, I will be there to hold your hand
and to ease your pain.
When you cry, I will be there to gently wipe the tears from
your eyes.
When you hug the pillow close to you because you feel so
much loneliness and so empty inside, I will be there to hold
you close.
When you are frightened because you don't know what
tomorrow holds, I will listen to you, and together we will
pray to the Lord to help you see the light once again.
My friend, in your darkest hour the Lord has heard you,
and tomorrow the sun will shine once again.
The Lord will lift the burden you feel tonight.
You will smile and love once again.
If you welcome the Lord with open arms, there is nothing
he wouldn't do for you.
Just ask, and if you believe, the Lord will give you more
than you bargain for.
When the Lord holds you in his arms, there will be no more
pain and no more sorrow.
He will take good care of you.
The Lord will lift your spirit so high there will be no more
darkness, only light.

The Blues

When you're feeling down and all alone and the blues just
won't go away, don't sit and cry.
Don't mope your life away.
Take control of your life.
Life goes on.
It's time to reevaluate your life.
Life is too short to keep on feeling sorry for yourself.
Don't sit alone in silence.
Call a friend,
take a walk,
get out and live your life, after all life is too precious to
waste.
You will see that once you decide not to waste another
moment and to start living your life to the fullest,
the blues go away.

Heartache

When I reach for you and you are not there, I feel the
heartache.
I hear you calling me.
I turn around, and you are not there.
I feel your tender touch and your warm embrace.
I close my eyes and I try to hold on to those moments for
as long as I can.
Throughout the day, I think of all the things I want to tell
you.
When I get home, I realize you are not there, and I feel the
heartache.
So many secrets I want to share with you.
The memories of you linger on and on.
There is not a day that goes by that you are not in my
heart.
My only consolation is that someday we will be together in
heaven, and then there will be no more heartache.

Open Up Your Heart

They look at you, but they don't see you.
They talk at you, but not to you.
They never make eye contact.
They talk about you like you are not even here.
Are you invisible?
You have a heart and a soul. You feel love and pain.
When you call for them, they ignore you. They say they are too busy.
They are always in a hurry.
You feel worthless because you are no longer productive.
You want to feel alive again.
You cry out, but they pretend not to hear you.
You feel like you are a burden.
When they visit, you feel like they are not really here.
They come because they think they have to, to put on a front.
They make you feel insecure.
They never hold your hand. They never show any compassion.
When you can't remember certain things, they act shocked.
They look at you like you have lost your mind.
They seem to be embarrassed to be with you.
You feel so lost.
You sit here all alone hoping that someday they will open up their hearts to you.
You want to be a part of them.
They have to remember, that even though you are up in years, you still have feelings and desires.
Your heart beats just like theirs.
You know you will continue to reach out to them, and maybe someday they will realize how much you love them.
You hope and pray that they will open up their hearts and let you in.

Time Slips Away

He told you he wanted to leave, that the spark had gone
out of your relationship.
You begged and pleaded for him to stay.
You know things have not been good for a long time, but
you are willing to try to work things out.
You have been together for a long time.
He says there is no fire in your relationship.
You know deep down in your heart that you can rekindle
your love.
You were busy with your careers and bringing up children.
Time passed, and you did not spend enough time together.
Time has a way of slipping by, where does the time go?
You are willing to try to make your relationship work.
He says you have grown apart, and he prefers to move on.
It hurts to see him go, but you wish him good luck.
You know that you will continue to love him always.

Loneliness

You sit in your room, rocking back and forth on your rocker.
You take out the photo album. You look at the photographs
and think back to the days when your family was all
together,
but now you feel so alone.
You take a sip of coffee as you look at the photographs.
You remember the good old days. Memories fill your heart.
You wonder where time has gone.
Your life is so empty now. You spend most of your days
alone.
Your dog jumps on your lap and licks your face.
Tears fill your eyes.
You remember when you were so busy you didn't even
have time to take a nap.
The house was always filled with family and laughter.
Now you have so much time on your hands.
You have noticed that you have less of an appetite
You are more frail and feel more fatigued.
You just don't have the energy to do much.
You wonder if a person can die of loneliness.
You don't want to confide in your family.
You don't want to burden them.
They are so busy raising their children and with their
careers.
You want to hold on to your independence for as long as
you can.
You wonder, how long you will be able to live in and main-
tain this big house?
How much loneliness can you endure?
You wonder if other people are as lonely as you.
You look out the window and see people busy everywhere.
You wonder why your life has to be so lonely. You reach for
the telephone.
Today you have decided to open up your heart and confide

in your family.
Today you will call a friend and stop dwelling in the good old days.
You will move on, start living, make new memories, and end this loneliness.

My Angel, My Friend

When I was feeling lonely in my new environment, you
came into my life and filled my heart with hope.
I knew from the moment I saw you that we would be
friends.
When I was in distress, I called your name, and you came
running.
You were always there to lend a helping hand.
You watched over me, and I will always be grateful.
Even though you could not help me, you held my hand and
spoke kind words of encouragement.
You touched my heart and soul.
When I was lonely, you sat by my side and kept me company.
Your positive attitude touched my heart.
Even though you are not here, I can feel your presence.
My Angel, my friend: can you hear the Angels call your
name, can you hear the birds sing, can you see the beautiful field of flowers, can you see the rainbows in the sky,
can you see all the beauty that surrounds you, can you
hear my voice thanking you for being my friend?

Friend

We were childhood friends.
We were four years old.
You spoke English.
I spoke Spanish.
We understood each other.
You had bisque dolls and store-bought toys.
I had handmade rag dolls and homemade toys.
You taught me some English words, and I taught you Spanish.
We colored books, played jacks, jumped rope, played hop-scotch, rode bikes, and climbed trees.
We spent all day together.
We had so much fun.
You moved away, and I was sad.
When I think of my childhood days,
I remember two little girls who were so different, yet had so much in common.

Elizabeth

Dear Elizabeth:
I am writing this letter especially for you.
I am sending it to heaven.
I know you are there with God and the Angels.
You were a kind, sweet, and loving person.
You were so easy to love.
When we prayed together, you held my hand.
When you looked at me, your eyes seemed to pierce right through my soul.
You always wanted me to reassure you that the Lord heard your prayers.
When we prayed, you told me that you felt so much peace in your heart, and that those were the times you slept so soundly.
We talked about the Guardian Angel.
I told you that God had sent a Guardian Angel to watch over you, and if you believed, you could feel the Angel's presence.
I am so happy that you trusted me to pray with you, and I could be there for you.
You were so afraid of the unknown.
Once you placed your trust in the Lord, you found peace.
When you opened up your heart to the Lord, it was so easy to make the transition.
You realized then that there never should have been any fear or anxiety, because the Lord had always been there for you.
Today I looked up at the sky, and I saw you smiling at me.
I saw your glowing face, you looked so peaceful.
I am so glad you finally found peace, and when the Lord called your name, you took His hand.

Love

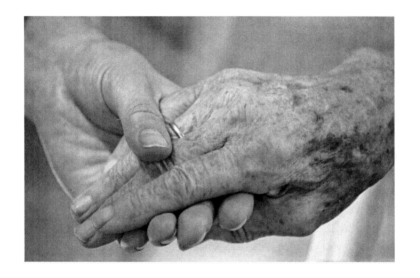

God gives
the special gift
of Love

The Meaning Of Love

Love is an emotion that comes from deep in the heart.
You can see it, and you can feel it.
The special things you do.
The smile that captures the heart.
A very gentle, tender touch.
Love is respect.
Love is caring.
Love is dependable,
makes you feel secure.
When you are in love, the sky is always blue,
feels like you are floating through clouds.
It is never stormy,
the sun is always shining.
You give, but never ask for anything in return.
You give flowers for no apparent reason.
The whole world seems to come alive.
You notice things that you have never noticed before.
You sing, you dance, and you feel like you are walking on air.
God gives the special gift of love.
Love is truly amazing.

I Love You

I loved you then,
I love you now.
Your tender kiss,
your sweet embrace.
You have given me more
than I have ever dreamed of.
What is life without your sweetness?
Without your love?
You give of yourself unconditionally,
we are like one.
You touch my heart,
my soul,
and my whole being.
I did not have to search for love.
God sent you to me, my love,
and I will love you always.

Happiness

Just knowing you are close by fills my heart with happiness.
Even when the days are cloudy, on gloomy days you make me happy.
When I am lonely, you build me up with kind words of encouragement.
Your honesty and your sincerity inspire me.
You have a way of lighting up my life with your smile, your touch, and your understanding ways.
I miss you when you are gone.
When I hear the car drive up the driveway, my heart skips a beat, because I know it's you.
The sound of your footsteps brings you closer to me.
Only one word to describe happiness, you.

I Admire You

When I saw you walking across the room, my heart
skipped a beat.
I knew we had to meet.
You smiled at me, what a radiant smile!
I smiled at you.
We started walking toward each other, and we met.
We dated and fell in love.
You asked for my hand in marriage,
I said, "Yes."
We have been together for many years.
Our love continues to grow.
We have so many things in common.
I admire your intelligence and positive attitude.
You are as thoughtful and considerate as you were then.
I adore you and cherish you.
Your patience overwhelms me.
I love you for just being you, and I know we will always be
soulmates.

My Love

My love, when I cried you wiped the tears from my eyes with your gentle touch. When I was insecure, you gave me confidence with words of wisdom.
When I was lonely, you were there to hold my hand and keep me company. When I was in pain, you made the pain go away with your tender touch and with comforting words.
When the day was dreary, you walked into the room with your sweet smile and your positive attitude.
You made my day!
When I was angry and took out my frustrations on you, you were so kind and never spoke an angry word.
You brought me flowers, gifts, and so much more.
You always did the right things to make me feel better.
You showed your love for me in so many ways.
You have touched my heart, my soul, and my whole being.
I treasure your love.

Together

I asked God to send me someone to love.
I was alone and feeling so lonely.
Everywhere I went I saw couples together, holding hands,
laughing, and just being together.
God sent you to me.
We have been together for a long time.
I love you as much today as I did then.
Everything is possible when we are together.
We set goals and make our dreams come true.
You have a way of saying the right things.
You are open and honest.
You wear your heart on your sleeve.
We walk through the flower garden, hand in hand.
We have sunshine every day, even when it's stormy outside.
Skies are never cloudy when I am with you.
I look at the sky, and I see rainbows.
God answered my prayers and made my dreams come true.
He sent me a special angel.

I Had a Dream

I had a dream you were here.
Your kiss on my lips was so soft and so sweet.
Your touch was light and so tender.
You ran your fingers through my hair, and whispered, "I love you."
Your smile intoxicated my heart and soul.
I was in a daze.
I felt like I was floating through the clouds.
My arms reached for you, and I whispered your name.
The air was filled with the smell of roses.
I could see your beautiful brown eyes and your olive skin.
My heart was beating fast.
My body seemed to be floating.
My arms were numb.
I felt like I could fly, but my body could not move.
You kept moving away and disappearing into the clouds.
I seemed to be moving right along, then I felt my eyes open.
I awoke, you were not there, and I knew it was only a dream.

Emptiness

Why does my heart feel so empty?
Why must I cry?
Where has the happiness gone?
I wish I could go back to happier days,
when you were here, my love.
You haunt my memories.
I see your face wherever I go.
I think of you constantly.
I don't seem to be able to let you go.
The world sees me as a happy person.
I do things I am supposed to do
each day, but my heart hurts deeply.
I can't seem to forget you, my love.
I have tried everything, but I don't
seem to be able to let go.
I can't sleep at night thinking of you.
When will this emptiness go away?
I know you have moved on, but I
don't seem to have the strength to go on.
I want to let go, but I can't.
Am I insane to continue wanting and
loving someone who does not want me?

You Are Special

My love, you are so special to me.
You go out of your way to please me.
You always put my needs ahead of yours.
You always remember birthdays and anniversaries.
You surprise me with gifts.
You compliment me every day, even when I don't look my best.
I think back to the day when we met.
It was a cold, cloudy, fall day.
I was hoping for some sunshine.
I was feeling blue.
I just wanted to be alone.
I had no desire to start a new relationship.
I was sitting on the park bench watching
the children play and people passing by.
I noticed that you were sitting on the bench across from me.
You came over and introduced yourself to me.
It was so cold!
You took off your jacket and put it around my shoulders.
How considerate!
Since that day, our love has grown.
We enjoy spending time together.
A walk in the park, listening to music, dancing, or just being together.
Thank you, my love, for being the special person in my life.
I treasure every moment we spend together.

I Dedicate My Love to You

Tonight I feel like crying for no apparent reason.
Tears of joy fill my eyes.
I grab a pen and a piece of paper.
I decide to write about how I feel.
You lie by my side,
I hear you breathing, and I hear your heart beat.
You are sleeping so soundly.
I want to dedicate my love to you.
I know that you think that I am strong, but you are the strong one.
You are my rock!
You are the only one who stands by my side through thick and thin.
When I am not sure of myself, you tell me how incredible I am, but you are the incredible one.
You tell me I am special, but you are the special one.
You are more than I ever expected in my life.
You look at me with so much love.
I love your smile and the way you talk.
I feel close to you, even when we are apart.
We share an incredible bond.
When I am away, I can't wait to get home to see your face and to feel your closeness.
I don't know what I have done to deserve someone like you.
Together we are a team.
We are an incredible couple.
God brought us together, and I am thankful.
I dedicate my love to you, my sweetheart.

A Dream

I woke up last night from a dream.
The dream seemed so real.
I reached for you, and you were not there.
I felt such emptiness.
I'm having such a difficult time adjusting to your absence.
I feel so guilty, because I wish I would have said, "I love you,"
more often, and spent more quality time with you.
Everything looks the same as when you were here.
So many memories flood my soul.
I felt so much love in my heart, but I did not express it often
enough.
Now that you are not here, I think back to the time when
everything was so wonderful.
My friends tell me that it takes time to heal and that soon I
will not feel so much loneliness, but my heart continues to
ache.
I vividly recall the dream I had.
A gate opened, and the stairs led up to a valley.
There were white doves flying everywhere.
The fields of wildflowers were so colorful and so fragrant.
I could see and hear water fountains, sounding like falling
rain.
I saw you standing by the fountains, you smiled at me.
You touched my hand and whispered, "Stop feeling so
guilty, my love.
You were such a wonderful companion, you showed true
love."
I looked up at you, and I felt like I could finally move on
with my life.

I Treasure

Some people treasure
silver and gold,
diamonds, emeralds, and rubies.
Collecting antiques, coins, and vintage wine.
I treasure family and friends,
a friendly smile.
A quiet evening at home.
A walk in the park.
The sound of the rain
falling against the window pane.
The smell of the roses.
I treasure your smile,
your tender touch,
your sweet embrace,
your soft kiss,
but most of all,
I treasure your love.

Wedding Anniversary

I knew it was going to be an incredibly romantic night.
I looked up.
You were standing there, looking so handsome.
My heart skipped a beat.
We reached for each other.
We embraced, and we kissed.
The lights were down low, you held me close.
There was no need for words, as we danced to the music.
Nothing seemed to matter as long as we were together.
The world outside did not exist.
We shared an incredible dinner, sat by the fire, and
exchanged gifts.
We got into the hot tub.
As we sipped champagne, we reminisced of our life
together.
When we met, I knew it was going to be a lasting relation-
ship.
The years passed.
We have loved each other, been companions and best
friends.
We have shared the good and the bad.
We have continued to be best friends.
Even in the most difficult times, we have remained strong
and in love.
We share unconditional love.
I want to thank you, my love, for this magical wedding
anniversary and for being the incredible person in my life.

I Am Free

God has given me wings.
I am free to fly like a dove.
Before I spread my wings and fly
I want to thank you:
for the love you gave me,
for always being there when I needed a helping hand, for
your compassion, your gentleness, and your consideration.
You cared for me with all your heart.
You gave of yourself unconditionally.
Your love was selfless, your love was true.
You made my life worth living.
Goodbye, my love,
Don't cry for me,
Hold the memories of me close to your heart.
Now I am free to fly
to the beautiful place
up in the sky.

No More Heartache

The time has come for me to close this painful chapter in
my life and let my heart rejoice.
The chains that have held my heart captive for so long
have been removed.
My heart has finally been set free.
No more heartache.
There is a warm feeling all over me that I can't describe.
Now that you are here with me once again, I will hold you
close to my heart and never let you go.
The blues are gone, my heart is singing, no more tears.
I feel like skipping and hopping like a child.
The whole world seems to be dancing with me.
You have captured my heart once again.

Don't Take Your Love Away

If you take your love away, you would certainly take away my reason for living.
Please don't break my heart.
Don't make me sad.
You light up my life every day, with your smile and tender touch.
Each day we spend together is like heaven on earth.
Nothing matters but the happiness you bring into my life.
You are the air that I breathe.
I know that without you, I would wither away.
Your love is like a beautiful dream that I don't want to wake up from.
Your love is like a bed of roses.
Your love takes me away to paradise.
You are the Angel that God sent from heaven to spend eternity with.

I Need You

Precious love, sweet love, you have taken my heart with you.
I don't know what to do.
You have left me all alone to cope with life's hardships.
What a heartache!
What will I do without you?
I have depended on your support for such a long time, now I am on my own.
I have no one to hold my hand and to tell me everything is all right.
So much silence.
I need to hear your voice and feel your touch.
Who do I turn to now, who do I confide in, who will listen to my problems at the end of the day, and who will tell me how wonderful I am?
I know I must move on.
Please give me a sign and tell me everything is going to be all right.

Your Love

Your love is endless, your love is true, that's for sure.
You give your love so freely it makes my heart skip a beat.
Your love is so gentle and sweet it takes me to a place I
have never been before, so high I can reach the stars.
Your love is so beautiful and pure like a rose after the
morning dew.
Your love is strong it keeps me sheltered from the storm.
Your love is plentiful, you give it with all of your heart.
When you love me, you give me the world, and that is
more than I have ever hoped for.
What can I say?
But thank you for your love.

Promise

I promise to love you forever, to be by your side until the end of time, to grow old with you, and to cherish your love.
When the night is long and you can't sleep, I will be there to hold you close to my heart.
When you need me, I will be there to open up my heart to you.
I promise to never leave you.
When you call my name, I will be by your side to listen to you, to hold your hand, and to let you know how much I love you.
I will treasure your love forever.
I will celebrate our love each day.
Nothing could ever stand in my way when it comes to loving you.
I promise to love you faithfully until eternity.

I Believe

There is a love that comes from deep in my heart, a love that lingers on day by day.
It comes from deep in my soul.
A special love that is only for you.
When you look at me and see that sparkle in my eyes, it's because I am thinking of you.
Even when I am not with you, I hold a special place in my heart for only you.
I believe that our hearts beat as one and that no one can come between us.
It is a bond that holds us together now and until eternity.
A love that makes me feel secure and that brings inner peace.
I can't imagine not having you in my life to love and to hold close to my heart.
Without you, there would be a void so deep I would not be able to stand the pain.
That is why I pledge my love for you today, to let you know that you make my life worth living.
With you in my life, every day is a beautiful day filled with so much happiness.
You make me smile and hum a tune, because that's what love does to me.
There is nothing more precious in my life than loving you.
You are my special Angel that keeps my heart singing.

When You Love Someone

When you give love and you never get love in return, it's the saddest feeling in the whole wide world.
When you love someone with all of your heart, you do all these special things, you give unconditional love, and you give that special smile, but that special someone acts like you don't exist.
You ask yourself, "What am I doing wrong?"
You feel so empty inside.
You feel like you could die.
You cry yourself to sleep, hoping that someday he will notice you.
You continue to dream of the day when he will look at you the same way you look at him.
You know that he might never love you, but you keep trying anyway.
Deep in your heart, you know that when two people love each other, there has to be that special bond.
You know that someday you will meet that special someone who will feel the same way you do.

Second Chance

I can't believe I could love again the way I'm loving you
right now and that I actually got a second chance at love.
I can't believe I opened up my heart to love.
Just when I thought that I would never find love again, you
came into my life, and my heart started singing once again.
When you took my hand in yours, I thought I was dreaming
when I felt the spark of love.
When you looked into my eyes, I thought it was a fantasy.
I felt a warm feeling come over me.
My heart was beating so fast, and that's when I knew it
was going to be a romance made in heaven.
I can't believe you took a second look at me.
You opened up your heart to me.
What a difference loving you has made in my life.
I am so glad I took a second chance at love.

Fly Away

I will fly away to the Promised Land.
I will fly over the mountains, valleys, meadows, lakes,
rivers, and parks.
I will leave everything behind.
I won't need material things.
No money, phone, nor jewelry.
I am going to a beautiful place where time stands still, so I
will not need a watch.
By day, I will follow the doves,
they will lead the way.
By night, I will follow the stars that twinkle in the sky.
My wings are my strength.
My hope and faith come from deep in my heart.
My courage comes from heaven above.
Farewell, my love.
Kiss me goodbye.
I have no regrets, because I have known your love.
Your love was my heaven on earth.
The memories of your sweet face will always live in my
heart.
I must go now.
The Angels will guide me to my destination,
where I will be free forever.

Key To My Heart

When you kissed me
it was the moment
I had been waiting for
for such a long time.
I heard my heart sing
it was a tune that
took my breath away.
I realized then that you
held the key to my heart.
The heavens opened up.
I heard thunder, even though
there was not a cloud in the sky,
and then a rainbow appeared.
It was then that I was certain
that our hearts would always
beat as one.
In my heart, I knew it was
not too soon to say, "I love you,"
because from that moment on,
I knew we would be together always.

Family

I will embrace
my Family
close to my
heart

My Family

There are millions of people in this world, but God gave me a circle of special people I call family.
Family is someone I can count on.
They are always there for me.
They make me feel important.
They give me confidence and encourage me to be the very best that I can.
When I feel like I am sinking, they gently guide me in the right direction.
They are never critical.
I never have to pretend to be anyone but myself, because they love me just the way I am.
They are always there to support me in my decisions.
When I fail, they are there to comfort me, to listen to me, and to encourage me to try again.
When I succeed, they are there to cheer me on and to congratulate me.
We are a strong unit that can never be broken.
We are not only family, but best friends.
I am never alone, because I have my family by my side.
I will embrace my family close to my heart, because they are the treasure that God sent from heaven above.
The beautiful memories we share each day will live in my heart forever.

Madre (Mother)

You sit by the window and wait for me. You know I will come. It breaks my heart because I am not able to be there for you more often.

Even though miles separate us, you are always on my mind and in my heart. Tonight I watched you sleep so peacefully, and I thought back to my childhood days.

You were there when I spoke my first word and took my first step. You were so proud. When I fell, you picked me up and wiped the tears. You comforted me with kind words of encouragement.

You were so patient. You walked me to school and held my hand. You gave me so much confidence. You showed love for your family on a daily basis. Your smile brightened my day. You waited for me after school, always had time to make me a special snack. You were always there to meet your family's needs with a smile.

You were there for every phase of my life, growing up and after. You showed love from the heart.

You were proud of all my accomplishments. When I failed, you were there to lend a helping hand. You never criticized me, even when I was rebellious. You understood my frustrations. You showed so much respect. You were always so positive.

You worried about my safety. When I had a bad dream, you let me sleep in your bed.

Even when times were difficult, you found ways to make it easier for me. When times were tough and the family was in crisis, you knew exactly what to do. You have gone through so much in your life. You have lost loved ones, friends; you are so strong. You have sacrificed so much. Even though I am grown now, I still need your admiration and respect.

I know I am who I am today because of your upbringing.

Let me hold your hand and let you know that I am here for you.

Today, I want to express my love and admiration for you. I want to thank you from the bottom of my heart for your love, patience, consideration, and respect.

I don't want time to slip away without telling you how I feel. I want the very best for you, and I want to do as much as possible to make your life a little easier. You have given so much to me.

I wake up every morning and think of you. I count my blessings because I have you. You are my special angel, and I treasure your love. Madre te amo (mother I love you).

Jefe (Dad)

You were my disciplinarian and my mentor.
At times, I resented your strict upbringing.
You brought me up with high moral standards.
You were always there for me.
You hardly ever said how you felt about me, but I knew
how much you loved me.
We were a big responsibility, but you worked and kept us
afloat.
I respected you.
You were stern and quiet.
As I got older, I noticed how your strict ways were gentle.
Time has come and gone.
I think back to when you were here.
You left so suddenly.
Life passes by, and we get older.
So much heartache and pain when you left us.
Many years have passed.
I miss you as much today as I did then.
We struggled through life,
you were there.
I wish I could have done more to make your life easier.
We don't know what we have until it is gone.
If only we could have yesterday again, relive life, and
change what has passed.
Life goes on.
We take the good with the bad; happy days, sad days,
aching hearts.
We love, and we hurt.
Many years have passed.
My life has changed, but my love for you remains the
same.

Daughter

There is no love more dear than the love between a mother and child.
It's a bond that lasts until eternity.
A woman awaits the birth of her child with anticipation.
When she looks into her child's eyes for the first time, she knows that God has given her the most precious gift in the whole world.
When I first saw you, my daughter, I knew that God had truly blessed me.
I held you close to my heart.
The joy I felt when you smiled at me was so overwhelming.
In my eyes, you were more than perfect, you were a gift from heaven above.
From that moment on, I knew I would never be alone.
You have always been an important part of my life.
You are a beautiful person with a kind heart.
You are a free spirit.
We have shared so many beautiful moments together.
I am so proud of you.
I care for you with all of my heart.
When I feel alone, I know that you are only a telephone call away.
It brings such joy into my heart, knowing that you are always there for me.
I thank God each day for your love, your patience, and for giving me such a special daughter.

Pocket Full Of Miracles

Dad was a farmer.
The crops had not done well that year due to the weather.
The season was over, and it was going to be a difficult winter.
Mom explained to the children about the difficult times to come.
The little children would have to wear hand-me-down clothes.
Mom would buy clothes at the thrift shop for the older children.
Mom bought material and patterns to make clothes.
She bought a pair of shoes for each of the children.
The children wore last year's jackets, which were kind of tight, but no one complained.
Mom canned fruits and vegetables.
Dad chopped wood to keep the house warm.
Dad said he would get odd jobs to make ends meet.
Mom was always busy; baking, sewing, cooking, and cleaning.
The children shared rooms.
We went to school every day. We studied together and did our chores.
We read books.
We made homemade ornaments for the Christmas tree.
All the gifts were handmade, but we were so happy.
Dad said, "Families that play and work together, stay together."
We had weekly family meetings.
One evening when we were gathered for the family meeting, Dad said, "It is going to take a miracle to get us out of this situation."
My younger brother reached into his jeans pocket and took out a little prayer book. He said, "I have a pocket full of miracles."

He handed the little prayer book to Dad.
We all read a prayer from the book of miracles.
The next day, Dad got employment.
Many years have passed, and I still think back to the little
book of miracles.

My Mission In Life

My mission in life is to make you happy.
When you are frustrated and discouraged with life, I will be there to hold your hand and encourage you. When you become angry with me, I will talk to you in a gentle voice, because I understand your situation.
I will be by your side on a daily basis to meet your needs.
My reward is your contentment and your smile.
I pray to God to keep me healthy so that I can be by your side when you need me.
When you cry, I will cry with you.
We will pray together to build up hope and faith.
Today is a beautiful day, as I enter your room you are asleep.
You open your eyes and smile at me.
You tell me you are not able to do much for yourself, but with encouragement you do so much.
I am so proud of you.
I want to build up your courage and confidence so that you can live your life the very best that you can.
At times, you tell me that you are old and worthless, but again I give you positive reinforcement.
We talk, we laugh, and we cry together.
We reminisce about the good old days.
You are a beautiful person inside and out.
You are my mother and my friend.
Don't ever doubt my love and my commitment to you.
I want you to feel secure in your environment and to know that someone is always there for you.
God has chosen me as your advocate, and I will do my very best for you.
I want you to be able to express yourself and to tell me how you feel.
My mission in life will always be your happiness.

Free At Last

You had struggled with your terminal illness for a long time.
You loved life and did everything possible to live.
Even though you had such a great burden to carry, you were always so positive and so full of hope and faith.
You were such a kind, sweet, patient, and considerate person.
You had a great support system.
You were loved.
Even when life got tough, you had such a good sense of humor.
You always said, "Everything will be all right."
You knew in your heart when there was nothing else you could do.
The night was calm.
You were surrounded by family.
God decided it was time to end your pain.
God came to you and held your hand.
God whispered, "My child, you have suffered enough.
Even in the toughest times you have shown so much hope and faith.
Don't be afraid, from now on there will be peace."
Tears filled your eyes.
You reached for your loved one's hand and speaking softly said, "Goodbye, my love. I love you with all of my heart and soul.
I know we will meet again someday."
The Angels smiled and said, "We will show you the way."
You closed your eyes and spoke calmly, "Jesus I am ready, take me home, my Savior."
You saw a light, and you heard music as you followed the Angels.
You felt so much peace as you entered the Kingdom of Heaven.
You were finally free.
You were home.

My Remembrance Of You

I remember your positive attitude,
your wonderful sense of humor, your sweet smile, and your
zest for life.
I can't remember a time when you were not here.
Now you are at peace and with God, my loved one.
Now that you are gone my heart is aching, my tears are
flowing, and my arms are empty.
Remembering you each day fills my heart with so much
happiness.
You brought so much joy into my life.
You had a green thumb.
Everything you planted multiplied.
God has chosen you to adorn the gardens in heaven.
You played the guitar so sweetly.
The Angels in heaven sing while you play the guitar.
I remember you with so much love.

I Feel Your Presence

How you loved the mountains.
Today as I looked up at the mountains I thought I saw your
face and you waving at me from the mountain top.
You loved the flowers, you loved to watch them grow.
Today as I worked in my flower garden, I reached over to
smell a rose. A rose petal fell into my hand, and I felt your
presence.
You loved the trees. They were so small when you planted
them in your yard, but with your tender loving care they
grew so tall.
Today I was sitting under the old oak tree. Leaves fell on
my shoulder, and as I reached to touch the leaves, I felt
your presence.
You loved to hear the birds chirp and watch the butterflies
fly about as you sat on your patio enjoying your morning
cup of coffee.
Today, a dove flew by and sat on the old wooden fence.
A butterfly flew by and landed on my arm.
I felt your presence.
You loved all living things.
Today, memories fill my heart as I think of you. You
inspired me in so many ways.
I don't know how far heaven is from here, but it must not
be too far, because you are always close by.
I feel your presence.

What A Sight

It was a spring day.
The sun was shining brightly.
The daffodils were in full bloom.
My eyes were filled with tears.
My heart was aching.
You were a little boy full of life.
God called your name.
The Angels surrounded you.
I heard the trumpet and the sound of music.
The gates of heaven opened up, and you entered the
Kingdom of Heaven.
It was such a beautiful sight.
My heart rejoiced.
God took your hand and led you through the gardens.
You looked so radiant!
You turned around and waved at me.
You gave me a smile.
Oh, what a sight to behold!
You disappeared.
You were home, my dear little brother.

This Road

This road is a long, wide, country road that seems so familiar.
I know I have traveled this road before.
Where does this road lead to?
On the side of the road grow many beautiful flowers: holly hocks, sweet peas, daisies, and so many colorful wildflowers.
I see butterflies flying about.
I hear the sound of birds.
Two rabbits quietly stare at me.
A groundhog pokes his head out of a hole.
I see fields of wheat and corn.
As I continue to walk, memories fill my heart.
I come to a gate.
I open the gate that leads to an old, white, frame house with a porch in the front.
The house seems so familiar.
I can almost hear the laughter of children.
As my mind wanders, I can see a dog with long floppy ears and a coat that looks like black velvet.
I can hear a gentle voice calling, "Supper is ready."
I can see a family sitting at the supper table holding hands.
The prayer is led by a handsome gentleman, with his eyes closed.
Even though this house is vacant now, it used to be a house filled with so much love and happiness.
A loving family resided in this house.
This road leads to the house that I grew up in and where memories were made. This house was home sweet home.

The Old Farm House

The old farm house was surrounded by oak and maple trees.
The wildflowers were so beautiful.
There were no neighbors for miles.
When I woke up in the morning I could smell coffee, biscuits, and hot cakes.
Mom was in the kitchen getting breakfast ready, Dad was getting ready for work, and my brothers and sisters were getting ready to start a new day.
The windows were open, and the air smelled so fresh.
I could hear birds chirping, a woodpecker building a home in the tree trunk, and squirrels running about.
My dog Bear and I would walk for miles, early in the morning.
We could see wheat fields, corn fields, rabbits, and groundhogs.
The sweet peas were so colorful and smelled so fragrant.
There was a swing on the front porch where I would sit and daydream.
The days were so peaceful, family working together and spending endless time together.
In the evening, Dad read passages from the Bible. The whole family would sing hymns.
I think back to those days out in the country.
The memories of the old farm house are so vivid.

If This Was My Last Day

If this was my last day on earth, I would call your name.
I would want you by my side to wipe the tears, because you would be the only one that would wipe them gently.
I would want you to hold my hand, so that I could feel magical vibrations flow through my body.
I would want to feel your tender kiss on my lips and your sweet embrace.
I would want to focus on your sweet face and outline your beauty in my heart to take with me to eternity.
I would want to hear your sweet voice that would sound like a choir of Angels singing.
I know that you would whisper gently to calm my fears.
You would be the one that would stop my heart from aching and reassure me not to be afraid of the unknown.
I know you would tell me of the beautiful things that await me, that God is waiting for me with open arms, that the Angels will lead the way, and that heaven is a beautiful place where there is no pain, only happiness.
You would say, "It's all right to go with Jesus."
Even though my tears would flow because I would not want to leave you, you would smile and say, "Be at peace, my love."
I know you would say all these wonderful things because I can depend on you.

> Your love is selfless,
> Your love is unconditional,
> Your love is true.

As I close my eyes, the last thing I see is your sweet face and your sweet smile.
I feel so calm as I drift into a place that is not familiar, but oh so comforting. Goodbye, my sweet Angel.
You are in my heart.
I love you.

Don't Cry For Me

Even though it seems like I am a million dreams away,
I watch over you.
When the rain falls, I am the raindrop that falls on your
head.
I am the rainbow that comes after the rain.
When the sun shines, I am the warmth you feel.
When you look up at the sky, I am the star that twin-
kles in the heavens.
I am the cloud that moves slowly across the sky.
When the wind blows, I am the breeze that gently rus-
tles your hair.
When the snow falls, I am the snowflake that falls on
your shoulder.
When you look up at the mountain, I am sitting at the
top looking down at you, watching over you.
I am the dream that you keep alive in your heart.
I am everywhere you are, even though you cannot see
me.
The memories of me that you keep in your heart keep
my spirit alive.
So don't cry for me, I am always close by.

The Adobe House

The adobe house was located at the bottom of a hill. The adobes were made by the whole family. They were made of clay like soil and straw. We shaped them like bricks and sun-dried them.

The house was warmed by a wood and coal furnace. Mom cooked our meals on a wood stove. We used kerosene lamps at night to do our school work.

All the children played on the hill. We had a lot of fun running up and down the hill. So many wildflowers grew on the hill. We would pick flowers and bring them home to Mom. She arranged them in a vase, and they added so much beauty to our home.

We made homemade toys to play with. My brothers made a wooden wagon and painted it red. We made trains out of sardine cans. In the winter we would sled down the hill. When we got home, Mom would have hot cocoa and gingersnaps waiting for us.

Mom grew beautiful geraniums and placed them on the window sill. Dad planted a vegetable garden. Mom canned the vegetables and stored them in the cellar. We all had chores to do before and after school. We raised sheep, goats, rabbits, pigs, and chickens. My brother and I would milk the goats. Dad made goat cheese.

Mom taught the girls how to cook, sew, crochet, and embroider at an early age. My sister and I would raffle crochet doilies.

We had no electricity, radio, or telephone. The family would sit by the fire and read books. We would converse with each other. We spend so much quality time together.

The sweet memories of my childhood days are so vivid. My heart aches for those days when life was so simple and so free.

Memories

Precious memories of you
from the bottom of my heart
make me cry
when I remember you:
your laugh, your smile, your voice,
your beautiful eyes, your sweet personality,
your gentle ways, and the beautiful
things you always did for your family.
Thoughts of the past years
when you were here
bring tears to my eyes.
I wish that you were here
so that I could tell you
that I love you
until eternity
and that I miss you
with all my heart.

Recuerdos (Memories)

Recuerdos preciosos de ti
del fondo de mi corazón
me hacen llorar,
cuando me recuerdo de ti:
de tu risa, tu sonrisa, tu voz,
tus ojos bellos, tu dulce personalidad,
tus modos suaves, y las cosas muy bonitas
que siempre hacías por tu familia.
Pensamientos de los años pasados,
cuando tu estabas aquí
traen lágrimas a mis ojos.
Yo quisiera que tú estuvieras aquí
para decirte que te amo
hasta eternidad
y que te extraño
con todo mi corazón.

The Voice

I heard a voice
at midnight.
I awoke.
I saw a light
that looked like a face.
I thought I was dreaming,
and what a surprise, it was you.
You smiled
and got close
to my bed.
You held my hand
and said, "I love you
with all my heart,
goodbye, my love."
I said, "I also love you,
and I miss you."
I cried out with joy.
You smiled and disappeared.
My heart cried out with pure happiness.
God made my dream come true.
I got to see you once more.

La Voz (The Voice)

Oí una voz
a la medianoche.
Me desperté.
vi una luz
que se parecía una cara.
Pensé que estaba soñando,
Y qué sorpresa, eras tú,
Te sonreíste
ye te acercaste
a mi cama.
Tú agarraste mi mano
y me dijiste, "te amo
con todo mi corazón,
adiós mi amor."
Yo dije, "yo también
te amo, y me haces falta."
Yo lloré de alegría.
Te sonreíste y te desapareciste.
Mi corazón lloró de puro gusto.
Dios hizo mi sueño verdadero,
te vi una vez más.

Take Care Of My Mother

God in heaven, please take care of my mother.
She is very kind, very precious, very beautiful, and a very
loving woman.
When she was on earth, I took care of her with all my heart.
Now I am very sad.
And my heart hurts very much,
because I miss:
her laugh, her hugs, and her kisses.
I cry everyday because I want to see my mother.
Sometimes at night I can't sleep, because I think she is
calling for me and
that she needs something.
I miss her with all of my heart.
Please God, take care of my mother for me.

Cuida A Mi Madre (Take Care of My Mother)

Dios en el cielo cuida a mi madre, por favor.
Ella es una mujer muy buena, muy preciosa, muy
hermosa, y muy cariñosa.
Cuando ella estaba aquí en la tierra yo la cuidaba, con
todo mi corazón.
Ahora estoy muy triste y me duele mucho mi corazón,
porque extraño: su risa, sus abrazos, y sus besos.
Todos los días lloro, porque quiero ver a mi madre.
Algunas veces en la noche no puedo dormir porque pienso
que ella me llama
o que ella necesita algo.
La extraño con todo mi corazón.
Dios por favor cuida a mi madre por mí.

Sisters

Sisters, my friends and confidants.
You are always here for me.
In times of crisis, we feel the same pain.
We join hands and hearts.
I can't imagine my life without you.
You listen to me without judging me.
Your patience overwhelms me.
You have always been there to share my happiness.
When I am sad or have a problem, you listen to me, and I
feel better.
You make me laugh.
I accept your advice with all of my heart, because I believe
in you.
I know that family is very important in our lives.
I don't know what I would do without you.
We are unique in our own special way, and yet we have so
many of the same qualities.
There is a special place in my heart for you.
God gave me sisters so that I will never be alone.
Thank you for your love and for always being here for me.

Hermanas (Sisters)

Hermanas, mis amigas y confidentes.
Siempre están aquí para mí.
En tiempo de crisis sentimos el
mismo dolor.
Unimos manos y corazones.
No puedo imaginar mi vida sin ustedes.
Me escuchan sin juzgarme.
Su paciencia me abruma.
Siempre están aquí para participar
en mi felicidad.
Cuando estoy triste o tengo un problema
me escuchan y me siento mejor.
Me hacen reír.
Acepto sus consejos con todo me corazón
porque creo en ustedes.
Yo sé qué la familia es muy
importante en nuestra vida.
No sé qué haría sin ustedes.
Somos únicas en nuestra propia
manera especial y
sin embargo, tenemos muchas de las
mismas cualidades.
Hay un lugar especial en mi Corazón
para ustedes.
Dios me dio hermanas para que
nunca estuviera sola.
Gracias, por su amor y por siempre estar aquí para mí.

Rose Mary

Rose Mary, the most beautiful rose in the rose garden.
Your beauty puts a dozen roses to shame.
You drive them insane, with your sophisticated ways.
All the roses wonder what makes you so unique.
Could it be your smile or your personality?
They try to imitate you, but you still shine above the rest.
You capture everyone's hearts with your charismatic ways.
All the roses in the flower garden finally came to realize,
that it must
be a gift sent from heaven above that makes the sun
always shine on you.
It definitely is your zest for life that makes you so unique.
I say there are many beautiful and colorful roses in this
world, but the most beautiful rose in this whole wide world
is my Rose Mary.

Memorial

Lord, it has been a very long and sad year since you took my mom home with you.
My heart has been burdened.
I have cried many tears.
It's very difficult for me to understand that I will never see my sweet Angel again here on earth.
I miss her smile, her voice, and most of all, her tender touch.
At times I don't think I can go on, but then you give me hope and faith.
You open up my heart and make it possible for me to believe:
that I will see mom again in heaven, that I will hold her hand once again, and that she will hear me say, "I love you," once again.
Lord, I know that mom is free from pain, no more sadness, and no more tears.
She is at peace.
I realize that mom is in a better place
where the Angels play the harp and sing, where the flowers bloom all year round, and where she can be with dad.
I am so happy that I got to spend a lot of time with mom.
It broke my heart to say goodbye.
It hurt so bad it took me by surprise.
Lord, thank you for giving me the most precious gift in the whole world, my mother.
Mom, until we meet again, I will hold you close to my heart.
The memory of you will live in my heart forever.

My Dog (Dale)

Where did you go, my loved one?
You left in the middle of the day.
No one saw you, and no one heard you.
I tried to keep you safe from your wandering ways.
I built a high fence, but you dug your way out.
I am searching for you.
I have spent many days and weeks looking for you.
Where are you, my loved one?
My heart is aching.
My life is empty without you,
will I ever see you again?
Everything reminds me of you.
I miss your smiling eyes, your floppy ears, and your wagging tail.
I hope you are safe.
I am so lost without you.
Everything remains the same, awaiting your return.
I pray to God to look after you.
You are loved and missed.

My Little Guy (My Dog Foley)

When I first saw you, I knew there was something special about you.
You ran around, curiously looking at me.
You only had eyes for me.
I loved you from the moment I laid eyes on you.
I brought you home, my little guy.
You filled the house with so much love.
You were always so playful and so curious of your surroundings.
You gave unconditional love.
I never had to do much to win you over.
You captured my heart, with that sweet shy look.
Today you put your wet, little nose on my cheek, you put your head on my lap, and you looked at me with those big brown eyes.
You are so perfect!
I never had to discipline you.
You always loved to please me.
You are such a good friend.
I hold you in my arms, and I know I must say goodbye.
I ask myself so many questions.
Did I do the very best for you? Yes I did!
Did I love you enough? Yes I did!
If I did anything but my best for you, I apologize from the bottom of my heart.
You were always so strong and so full of determination, now you have lost your strength and are getting weaker.
I have so many wonderful memories of you.
You hold a special place in my heart.
The time has come for me to say goodbye. I don't want to let you go.
My life will be empty without you.
I only want the best for you.
My sweet Angel, close your eyes and go to eternal rest.

Prayer

The Lord
gives me
inner peace

In The Hands Of The Lord

I put my life in the hands of the Lord.
He is the one that I trust.
Even before I call his name, he is by my side.
When my life is in crisis and I don't seem to be able to cope with life's hardships, I feel his presence.
When the Lord puts his hand on my shoulder, I feel like I can move mountains.
When I am troubled and everything in my life seems to be more than I can handle, I know I can put my hope and faith in the Lord.
I know he will never let me down.
When I feel so empty inside, the Lord gives me inner peace.
I am so glad I put my life in the hands of the Lord.

I Will Walk With You

I will walk with you until the end of time.
I will wait for you in heaven and walk hand in hand with you.
My promise to you, my love, is that no matter what the circumstances, I will be there for you.
If you fall, I will be there to pick you up.
I will carry you for miles on my shoulders to safety.
Just call my name, and I will come running to you.
When you hurt, I will feel your pain, and I will comfort you.
When you cry, I will wipe the tears from your eyes.
When you are cold, I will wrap my arms around you to keep you warm.
When you are thirsty, I will bring you a glass of water to quench your thirst. When you are sick, I will be by your side, to sit with you, to comfort you, and to hold your hand. Nothing in the world could keep me from walking hand in hand with you.
I will be there for you, to walk by your side forever.

An Angel

I looked up at the sky and saw a traveling cloud.
The cloud looked like a giant marshmallow.
I watch for several seconds, and inside the cloud I could
see a glowing face.
The most beautiful sight I had ever seen!
Suddenly I saw an Angel beckoning to me.
The Angel was calling my name. I cried out with joy.
The Angel came down, touched my hand, and whispered,
"You were chosen." I knew then that my journey here on
earth was over and my eternal journey had begun.
I climbed on the Angel's wings.
As we traveled through the clouds, I felt as light as a
feather.
I felt no fear, only contentment. A bright light was shining
up ahead. I could hear beautiful music, sounded like the
harp.
All of a sudden the gates of heaven opened up, and I knew
I was HOME.

Miracles

Jesus, I would climb the highest mountain on my hands and knees to show my love for you.
You have given me so many miracles.
I don't know what I have done to deserve all your kindness.
When I don't think I can go on, you are there to lift my spirit, with open arms.
When I am down and all alone, you stand by my side.
I ask myself, *"Who am I to deserve someone who believes in me the way that you do?"*
Only you, Lord, are so forgiving of all my shortcomings.
I could not sleep last night, my heart was so burdened.
I awoke this morning, and you granted me yet another miracle.
You are so good and pure.
Please make me worthy of your love.

My Personal Angel

God sent me a personal Angel to watch over me.
My angel walks by my side and keeps me safe, guides and protects me.
When I have a problem, my Angel helps me solve it.
When I get up in the morning, when I am at work, when I am tempted to do the wrong thing, my Angel is there.
My Angel helps me to make the right decisions, helps me to be kind and considerate toward others, and keeps me from having a negative attitude.
When I am sick, my Angel comforts me.
When I drive down the highway, my Angel sits by my side and watches over me. My Angel brings me luck.
When I am about to make a mistake, my Angel taps me on the shoulder and reminds me to do the right thing.
When I can't sleep at night, my Angel reminds me to say a prayer, and I fall asleep.
My Angel keeps me from evil temptations.
I can't see my Angel, but I feel my Angel's presence.
My Angel is a GUARDIAN ANGEL.

Pardon Me, Lord

Pardon me, Lord, for not believing in you and for losing
hope and faith.
When my life was in crisis, I was feeling all alone and felt
that I had no one to turn to,
I gave up and did not trust in you.
In the past you have always been there for me.
I should have known that you were by my side and that
you would show me the way.
Pardon me, Lord, for doubting you.
Thank you for opening my eyes and showing me the way.

Call On Me

Lord, keep me strong in health, heart, and spirit so that I can be helpful to others.

> To be considerate
> To be compassionate
> To show empathy

Help me to make someone's life happy.
> To listen
> To hold someone's hand
> To brighten someone's day

with a hug, touch and a smile.

If someone is less fortunate than me, let me share the many blessings that you
have given to me.

Help me to be selfless.

I want to open up my heart so that I can be called on when someone is lonely or
not felling well.

Lord, make me that person who can be dependable, because Lord the most
wonderful things in life, money can't buy.

> Love
> Trust
> Respect
> Happiness

We are here on earth for such a short time.
Lord, make me that person that others can count on.
I want to leave this earth knowing that I have made a differ-
ence.

I Hear You Calling

Jesus, I hear you calling for me.
The Guardian Angel you sent to watch over me takes such good care of me.
The Angel wipes the tears from my eyes, cleanses the sweat from my brow, holds my hand, and makes sure I am free from pain.
Jesus, I can't open my eyes.
I don't seem to be able to focus on what is happening around me.
I hear voices, sounds like the voices of my loved ones.
I hear crying.
Jesus, please help my loved ones to cope with my absence.
Let them know that it is all right to mourn, but to move on with their lives.
Jesus, I have followed the Ten Commandments.
I have lived my life the best that I can.
If I have sinned, please forgive me.
Have mercy on me.
I open up my heart to you, my savior.
Please cleanse my soul.
Jesus, I know that I am getting weaker.
I am feeling calmer.
I feel no pain.
I feel so much happiness.
I see the gates of heaven open up.
I see Angels, and I hear music.
The sound of the harps are so soothing.
I am drifting, drifting.
Jesus, I hear you calling for me.

Empty Shell

Jesus, without you by my side, I am nothing but an empty shell.
You walk by my side and guide me in the right direction.
You fill my heart with love and my life with hope and faith.
When my body is weary and the whole world seems to be against me, when I see no light only darkness, you are there for me.
Your firm, gentle hand keeps me on the right path.
You are my salvation.
Jesus, you hear my cry, you see my tears, and you feel my pain.
You turn my weakness into strength.
You help me overcome my insecurities, and you give me patience beyond belief.
I worship you, for you alone can fill this EMPTY SHELL.

Remember Me

When God opens the gates of heaven and calls for me, I
will be ready.
I will go with dignity to eternal rest.
We have shared many wonderful times, made many mem-
ories.
I have lived many wonderful years.
The time has come for me to leave this earth and enter the
kingdom of heaven.
Don't shed too many tears.
Move on with your lives, be happy.
Remember me with a smile, with love.

Embrace Me, Lord

Embrace me, Lord, and make me worthy of your love.
Some days it is hard to follow the right path.
In my heart I know I only want to do the right thing.
If I have failed in the past, I open up my heart today.
I ask for forgiveness.
I get down on my knees and worship you, for you are the one who has given me life.
Life is a long, hard road with many mountains to climb.
You are here by my side every day.
You watch over me, guide and protect me.
I feel your presence every day as I go about my life.
When I stumble and fall, you give me strength to get up and continue on.
When I cry because I have lost hope and faith, you give me courage.
When I am exhausted, you give me strength.
When I think all doors have closed, you open up doors of opportunity for me.
You work in mysterious ways.
Lord, grant me the strength to know right from wrong and to live my life the very best that I can.
Lord, I feel your hand guiding me toward the right path.

God Called My Name

I awoke to the sound of music.
I opened my eyes and saw a bright light.
I saw four snow-white doves flying about.
I thought I was dreaming when I saw God.
God called my name.
The Angels surrounded me.
The Angels whispered, "We were sent by God to take you home."
Oh! What a sight to behold.
I cried out with pure joy.
I looked around me and saw the faces of my loved ones.
They smiled at me as they held my hand and kissed me on the forehead.
I saw tears in their eyes.
I whispered, "Please don't cry, I love you, we will meet again someday."
I closed my eyes.
As I walked through the gardens of paradise, I felt so enlightened.
Oh! What peace I felt when the gates of heaven opened up and I was finally home.

Life

Jesus, life is like a roller coaster, so many ups and downs.
Please help me to stay on the right track.
Some days the road I travel is so long and rocky, the
mountain I climb is so steep, and the load on my shoulders
seems so heavy.
I feel your gentle hand guiding me.
You lift the weight off of my shoulders, and you make it
possible for me to go on.
When my heart is heavy and my body is weary, you come
to my rescue and give me the strength I need to go on.
When I cry because I am impatient and have lost faith, you
open up my heart and let me see the wonders of life.
Jesus, I am so grateful for the love that you show for me.

High On Life

Jesus, thank you for this new day.
I give thanks for the many wonderful things in my life and for the beauty that surrounds me.
I am happy to be alive.
My heart is filled with so much gratitude for all you offer to me each day.
The day is open to so many possibilities and excitement.
As I look out the window I see:
The green grass and the beautiful flowers.
The roses, sweet peas, and morning glories.
The wonderful scents of the flowers overwhelm me.
I hear the birds chirping outside, what a beautiful sound!
I see my loved one's beautiful smile, it means the world to me.
The sight of the children playing outside is such a beautiful sight.
I love to see my dog running about so playful.
Each day is so special.
I want to treasure every moment.
Jesus, I feel so blessed to be able to enjoy all the beauty around me.
I AM HIGH ON LIFE.

On The Angel Wings

I am riding on the Angel wings, to a peaceful place up in the sky.
Where there are no more mountains to climb, no more schedules to meet, no more problems to solve, no more sickness, no more pain, no more sadness, and no more tears.
As the Angel spreads her wings and we continue our journey, my heart is rejoicing.
I can only imagine the beauty that awaits me.
Don't cry for me, my loved ones.
We shall meet again in that beautiful place in the sky where we will walk hand in hand through paradise.

Angel

An Angel came to me in my time of need.
I was feeling so lost, so overwhelmed with life, and so
tired.
Since God took you away from me, I felt I could not go on.
The Angel touched my hand, wiped the tears from my
eyes, whispered words of kindness, and comforted me
with words of encouragement.
The Angel seemed to know exactly how I felt.
I reached for the Angel's hand, my heart felt so enlightened
and so full of hope.
I confided in the Angel about my troubled life and how I
had lost hope and faith.
The Angel listened to my every word without judging me.
The Angel was so kind and considerate.
All of a sudden, I felt the weight being lifted off my shoul-
ders.
I felt inner strength that I had not had for such a long time.
I felt like I could move mountains.
    I heard music.
    I started to sing.
The Angel whispered to me, "There are no more moun-
tains to climb."
I looked up at the Angel and realized the Angel was you.

The Right Path

I am very emotional today.
I know that it is not very becoming to be angry.
I know that life is a struggle and that there are many trials
in a person's life.
Jesus, make me strong.
Help me to make the right decisions.
I want to prove to you that I am deserving of your love.
Help me to learn from my mistakes.
Tears flow from my eyes, and as I wipe the tears I think of
all the times you have been there for me.
Please cleanse my heart and soul.
Help me not to expect perfection of myself and others.
Jesus, I pray to you from my heart.
Please keep me from straying in the wrong direction.
Keep me going on the right path.

We Will Lead You Home

The Angels joined hands and formed a circle around my bed.
One Angel sat down on a chair by the bed and held my hand, while another Angel cleansed my face with a cool, moist cloth.
The Angels whispered comforting words.
I heard music not too far from my bed.
I opened my eyes and saw an Angel playing the harp.
Another Angel was singing softly and tenderly, "We will lead you home."
I could not keep my eyes open and could no longer focus.
I could not verbally express myself.
My heart was filled with so much love and a wonderful feeling of contentment.
I felt no pain.
I knew I was drifting into a state of unconsciousness.
I felt the Angel's hand on mine.
The Angel whispered, "We were sent by God to lead you HOME."

I Am Thankful

Lord, show me the way, so that I will not stray from what is important in life.
I woke up this morning feeling so tired, so lonely, and so overwhelmed with life. I did not want to get up.
I thought, *"What's the use?"*
It's just another day.
I had such a negative attitude.
I pulled the covers over my head and closed my eyes.
All of a sudden, I thought I felt someone's presence.
I look around but could not see anyone.
I felt such strength come over me.
I felt like the weight had been lifted off my shoulders.
I got up and opened the window shades.
The sun was shining brightly.
I looked out the window.
The flowers in the garden looked so beautiful and so colorful.
I could smell the scent from the roses.
The day was filled with promise.
My spirit was lifted.
I got down on my knees and gave thanks for all the beauty that surrounded me. Lord, you have given me so much to be thankful for: my health, loved ones, and a great job.
Thank you for being there for me and lending me a helping hand.
Thank you for letting me see that even though life is not perfect, there is so much to live for.
Lord, in the future I will close the door to all negative thoughts and open up my heart to what's important in life.

Lead Me Home

Lord, help me not to be bitter of my situation.
Help me to be strong.
Help me to be accepting and not to take out my frustrations on others.
I want to give thanks to all the people around me who are so caring.
Loved ones who stand by me no matter what the circumstance may be.
I close my eyes and think back to all the wonderful things in my life, so many wonderful memories which I will take with me.
Lord, help me to keep on smiling, to speak gently to others, and to reach out with open arms to all my family and friends.
Give me strength, especially at night when the lights are out and my mind tends to wonder.
I start to think of my situation and what could have been.
The only thing that matters now is that I prepare myself for the journey ahead of me and for you, my Lord, to accept me as one of your children in the kingdom of heaven.
Tonight, I saw a vision.
I saw Angels all around me.
I heard music, I saw a light shining close by.
I know the time is near.
I feel your presence.
Lord, take my hand and lead me home.

Stairway To Heaven

The Angel said, "There is a stairway that leads to the gates of heaven.
In order to get to the top, you have to start at the bottom.
Not everyone makes it to the top. Take one step at a time.
It takes work and determination. You may start your journey now.
You will encounter many hardships along the way.
Don't give up." I looked at the steep stairs.
I did not think I could make it to the top.
I knew that the journey ahead would be rocky.
The Angel said, "When you get tired and the journey gets tough, you need to show your strength, courage, and determination.
Remember, there will be days when there will be no sunshine, only darkness."
I continued to climb. I felt like I had climbed stairs for days.
I was so exhausted.
When I got to the top stair, I saw a gate, and the gate opened up.
The Angels welcomed me and led me through the gate.
The beauty was beyond belief. I saw God and all the apostles.
I saw loved ones that had crossed over.
God said, "You have traveled so many miles.
You have fulfilled your mission. You have met all the requirements.
This is the kingdom of heaven. This is your home."
I felt so excited and cried out with joy and happiness.
I reached over to touch God's hand, but I could not feel anything.
My fingers were numb. I heard music.
The Angels played the harp and sang.
I tried to sing along, but I had no voice.

My feet were not on the ground. I was floating.
I felt as light as a feather. I felt like I had wings.
All of a sudden, I heard the alarm clock go off.
I awoke from a deep sleep. I knew I had been dreaming.

Take My Hand

Lord, when you call for me, I will welcome you with open arms.
I know that I am here on earth on borrowed time.
When I hear the Angels whisper my name and see the gates of heaven open, I will reach out for you, my Lord.
My heart will rejoice.
I will not be sad.
I will leave with a smile, because the beauty and joy I will encounter when I see you, my Lord, will be beyond belief.
When the time comes, take my hand, Lord, and lead me home.

My Angel

There is an Angel in heaven who watches over me.
She knows exactly how I feel.
When I am sad, she brightens my day.
When I am afraid, she gives me courage.
When I am weak, she gives me strength.
My Angel can look into my heart and soul.
My Angel knows when I feel insecure.
My Angel helps me to believe in myself.
My Angel tells me to spread out my wings and fly.
I believe in my Angel, and my Angel believes in me.

Lord

The Lord has blessed me.
He has taken me in his arms and held me close to his heart.
He has given me wings to fly; now I can soar like an eagle.
I am free.
He has given me peace in my heart.
He has taken all the sadness out of my life.
Now I can smile again.
I have regained hope and faith, and I can believe once again.
I can trust again and open up my heart to others.
No more heartache, only happiness.
I have wasted so much time, now I can start to live again.
Gentle Lord, thank you for watching over me.
You have truly blessed me.

The Lord Called My Name

Oh, what joy I felt when the Lord called my name.
I could not believe that the Lord was calling me.
I turned around, and he was standing there.
I was so overjoyed.
I knelt down at his feet and praised him.
I cried, "Lord, I am not worthy of your love."
The Lord took me by the hand and lifted me up.
He wiped the tears from my eyes.
We walked hand in hand until we reached the most beautiful place I have ever seen.
I heard music, and then I saw the Angels.
I felt such peace as the gates of heaven opened up, and the Angels welcomed me home.

My Prayer

My prayer is that the Lord will be with you in your time of need and that he will watch over you day and night.
I asked the Lord to send an Angel to watch over you, to ease your worries and pain.
Once you're in the Angel's arms, you will feel the peace that the Lord has intended for you.
Don't be afraid to open up your heart to the Lord.
Take the Lord's hand in yours, and he will lead you in the right path.
He will guide and protect you.
Today I saw you, and I knew that my prayers had been answered.
You looked so peaceful.
You told me that your worries were over, that you were free from pain, and that you had accepted the Lord.
Just remember that I am here for you for as long as you need me, to keep you company, and to assist you in any way I can.
I know that you will never be alone as long as you have the Lord by your side.

FLORIDA VIGIL is a native of the beautiful state of Colorado. She was born in Trinidad and grew up in the southeastern town of Swink, Colorado.

Florida attended nursing school in Westminster, Colorado. She currently lives in Denver with husband, George, and beagle, Sadie. When not writing, Florida enjoys working as a nurse and spending time with family and friends. Some of her hobbies include gardening, cooking, reading, walking, hiking, playing the guitar, and singing.

Writing poetry inspires Florida to feel thoughts and fuels her imagination. She writes what she feels in her heart; thoughts, emotions, and dreams that transpire into poetry. She not only writes about her own dreams and life experiences, but also what she feels other people experience in their lives and relationships.

As she writes, she opens up her heart and imagines what other people feel; their happiness, heartaches, pain, and tears. She can see their smiles and hear their laughter. She believes that writing encourages her to be more observant of the world.

LaVergne, TN USA
09 July 2010
188999LV00005B/2/P